Mick Manning
and Brita Granström

Beaks and Feet

Illustrated by
Mick Manning

OXFORD
UNIVERSITY PRESS

OXFORD
UNIVERSITY PRESS

Great Clarendon Street, Oxford, OX2 6DP, United Kingdom

Oxford University Press is a department of the University of Oxford. It furthers the University's objective of excellence in research, scholarship, and education by publishing worldwide. Oxford is a registered trade mark of Oxford University Press in the UK and in certain other countries

Text © Mick Manning and Brita Granström 2014

Artwork © Mick Manning 2014

The moral rights of the authors have been asserted

First published 2014

All rights reserved. No part of this publication may be reproduced, stored in a retrieval system, or transmitted, in any form or by any means, without the prior permission in writing of Oxford University Press, or as expressly permitted by law, by licence or under terms agreed with the appropriate reprographics rights organization. Enquiries concerning reproduction outside the scope of the above should be sent to the Rights Department, Oxford University Press, at the address above.

You must not circulate this work in any other form and you must impose this same condition on any acquirer

British Library Cataloguing in Publication Data
Data available

ISBN: 978-0-19-830811-9

10

Paper used in the production of this book is a natural, recyclable product made from wood grown in sustainable forests. The manufacturing process conforms to the environmental regulations of the country of origin.

Printed in China by Golden Cup

Acknowledgements

Series Editor: Nikki Gamble

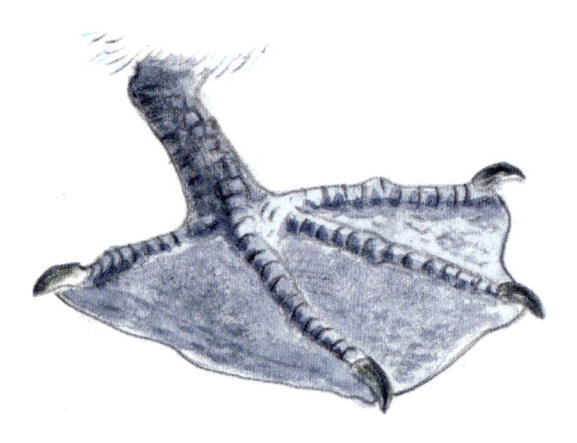

Which feet go with the beaks in this book?

This book is all about beaks and feet.
Can you guess who the beaks belong to?
If you read to the end, you might get a surprise …

Contents

Whose Stripy Beak Is This?	5
Whose Hooked Beak Is This?	9
Whose Long Beak Is This?	13
Whose Pointed Beak Is This?	17
Whose Beak Is This?	21
Glossary and Index	24

4

Whose Stripy Beak Is This?

This stripy beak belongs to an Atlantic puffin.

These small seabirds spend autumn and winter at sea and only visit land in spring and summer to **breed**.

In the **breeding season**, puffins look very smart with brightly-coloured beaks and orange feet. In autumn and winter, the colours of their beaks and feet fade.

Puffins have **webbed feet**. This helps them swim underwater, where they catch small fish to eat. They have large beaks which can hold many fish in a neat row.

To make a nest, puffins dig **burrows** in the soft soil of islands and cliff tops. The female lays a creamy-white egg in the burrow. This soon hatches into a hungry chick called a puffling.

A puffling needs to be fluffy and fat to keep warm.

parent

puffling

When pufflings are about six weeks old they leave the nest. They jump into the sea to join their parents ... **PLOP!**

7

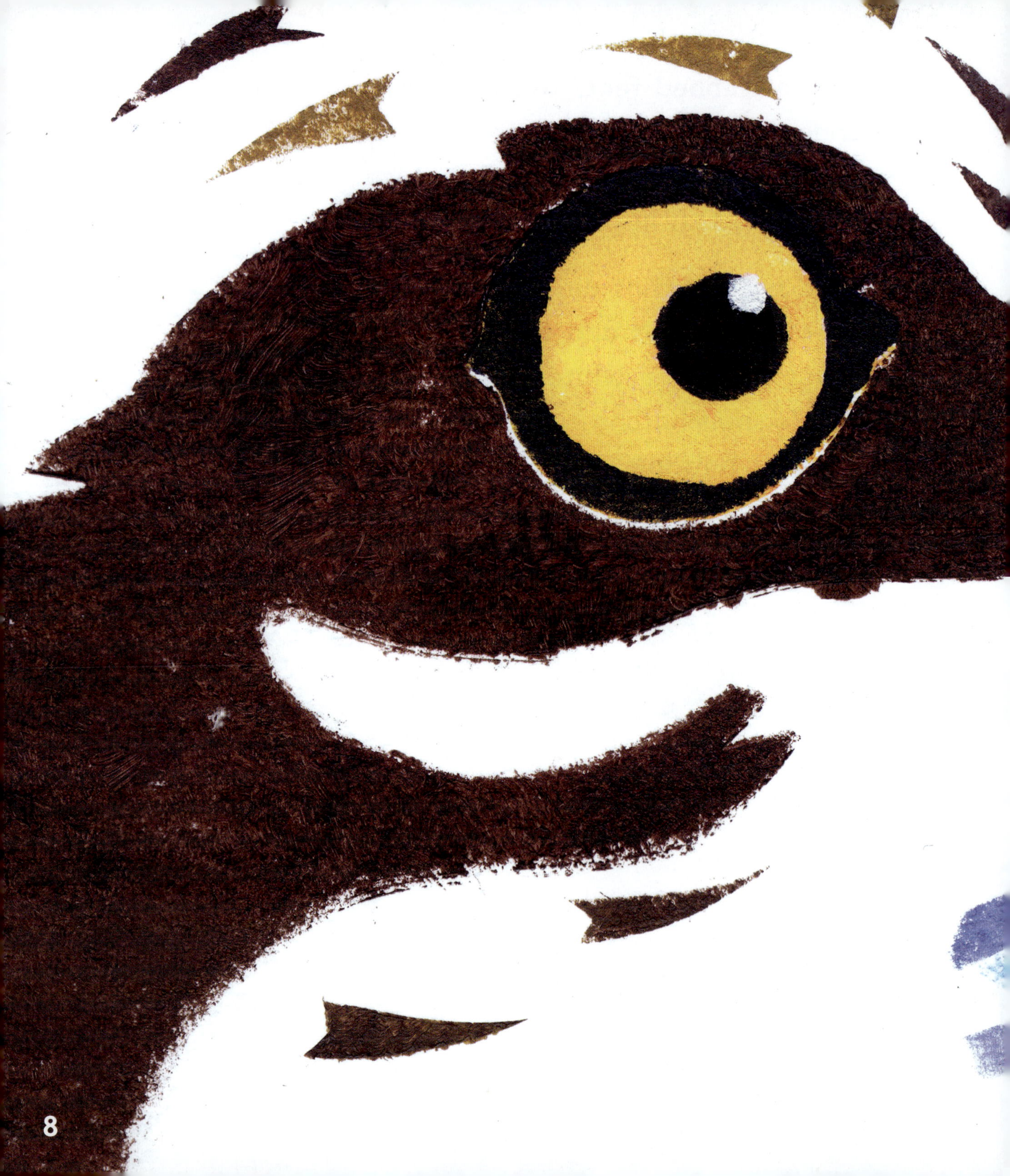

Whose Hooked Beak Is This?

This hooked beak belongs to an osprey.

Ospreys are large **birds of prey** that eat fish. They hover above the water, then dive in like feathery arrows ... SPLASH!

Ospreys have powerful feet with very sharp claws called talons. They use their talons to catch and hold on to the slippery, wriggly fish.

Ospreys live in almost all parts of the world, from America to Australia. Some ospreys fly long distances to spend the winter in Africa. This is called **migration**. Other ospreys, such as the ones that live in Australia, stay in one place all year round.

This mother osprey has a nest with two chicks. She is feeding them tasty chunks of fish.

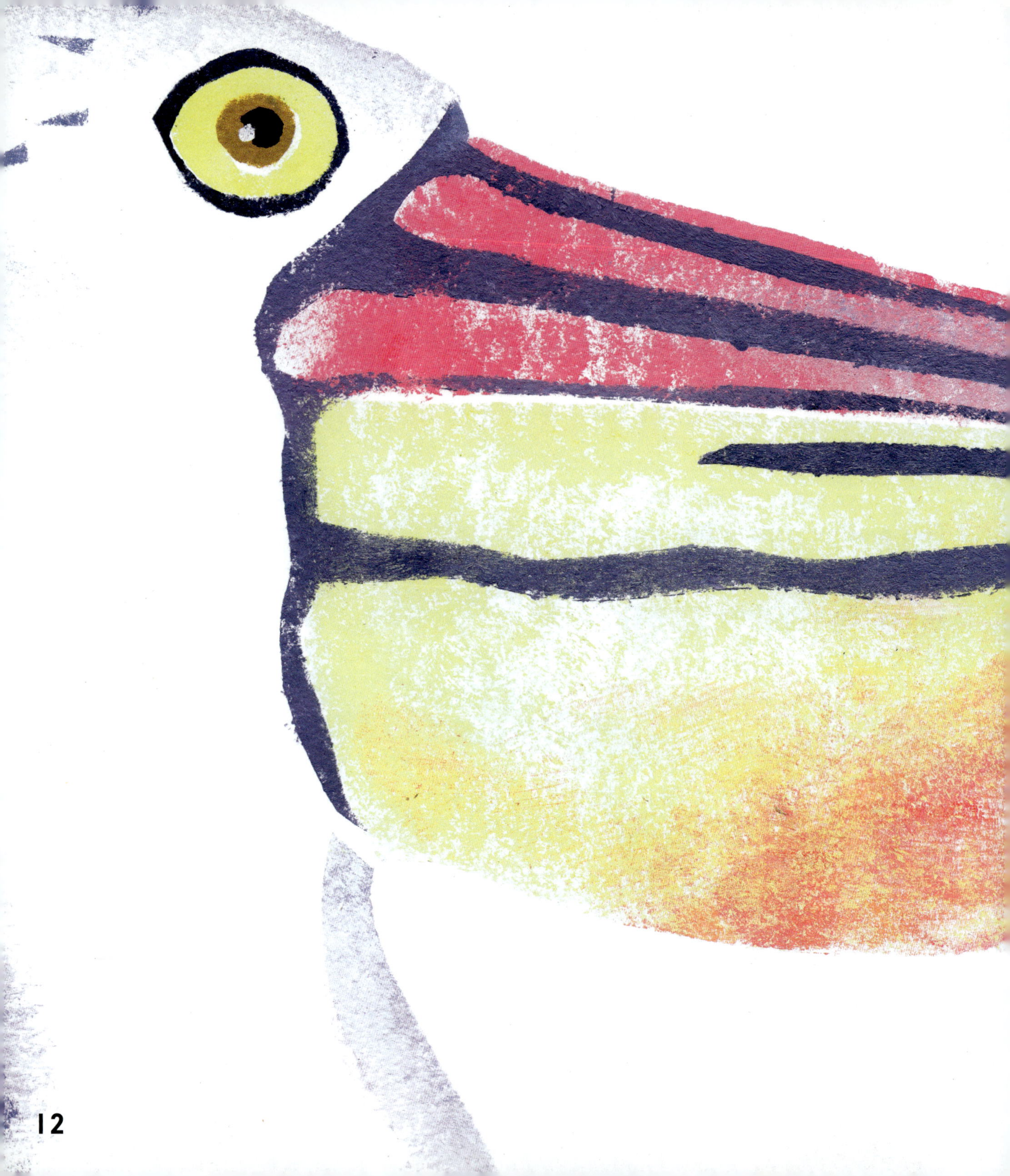

Whose Long Beak Is This?

This long beak belongs to an Australian pelican.

A pelican's beak is also called a bill. Pelicans feed mostly on fish but they also eat frogs and crabs. Some types of pelican plunge underwater to catch their **prey**. Others scoop up food from the surface.

When a pelican feeds, the pouch of skin under its bill stretches to scoop up water and fish. Then, as the water drains out, the fish are trapped inside ...

GULP!

Pelicans have large webbed feet for paddling. Their feet are also good for walking in mud and sand.

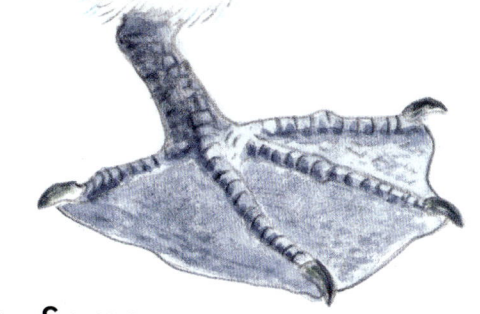

Pelicans nest in groups called **colonies**. Some pelicans, such as the Australian pelican, nest on the ground. Other types of pelican nest in trees.

This mother pelican is feeding her chicks.

Pelican chicks are born without feathers. As they get older, Australian pelican chicks gather together in 'pods' of up to 100 chicks to stay safe from **predators**. The parents can recognize their own chicks at feeding time!

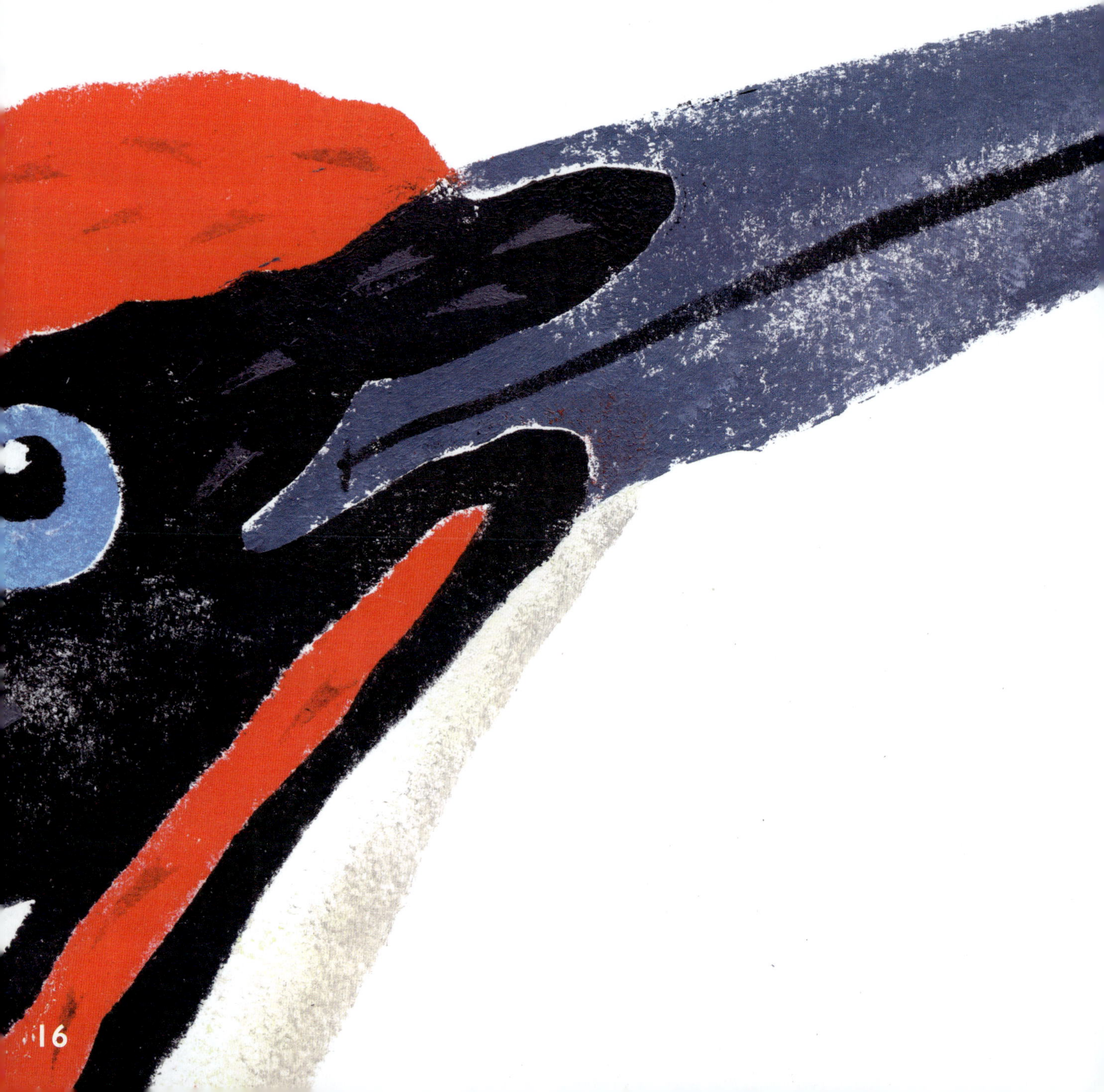

Whose Pointed Beak Is This?

17

This pointed beak belongs to a
green woodpecker.

Woodpeckers usually live in woodland and forests. They use their beaks to dig out and eat the beetle grubs that live under tree bark and in rotten wood. They also eat fruit, nuts and **sap**.

Woodpeckers peck out tunnels to make their nests in tree trunks. The females lay around four eggs in the nest.

TAP!

TAP!

TAP!

Unlike many forest birds, woodpeckers can't sing. Instead, they communicate with other woodpeckers by tapping very fast on trees, poles or even chimneys. This is called drumming.

great spotted woodpecker

There are lots of different types of woodpecker.

black woodpecker

pileated (say pigh-lee-ay-tid) woodpecker

Woodpeckers have strong skulls and muscles. This stops them getting hurt when they are drumming. Woodpeckers also have long, sticky tongues. Their tongues reach inside holes to get at beetle grubs and ants' eggs.

tree trunk

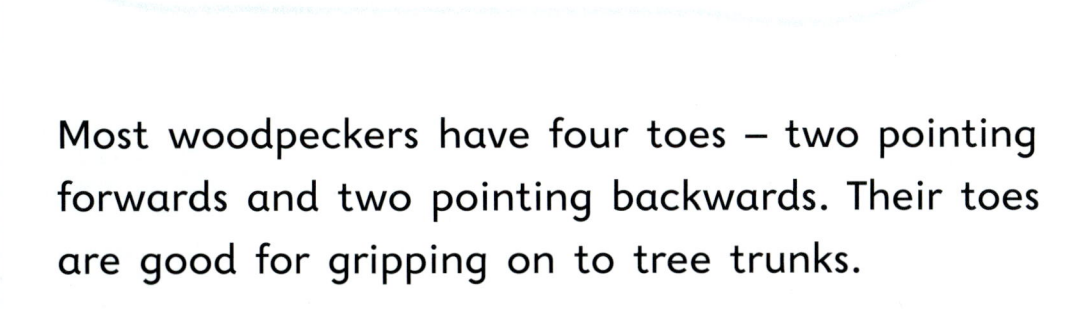

Most woodpeckers have four toes — two pointing forwards and two pointing backwards. Their toes are good for gripping on to tree trunks.

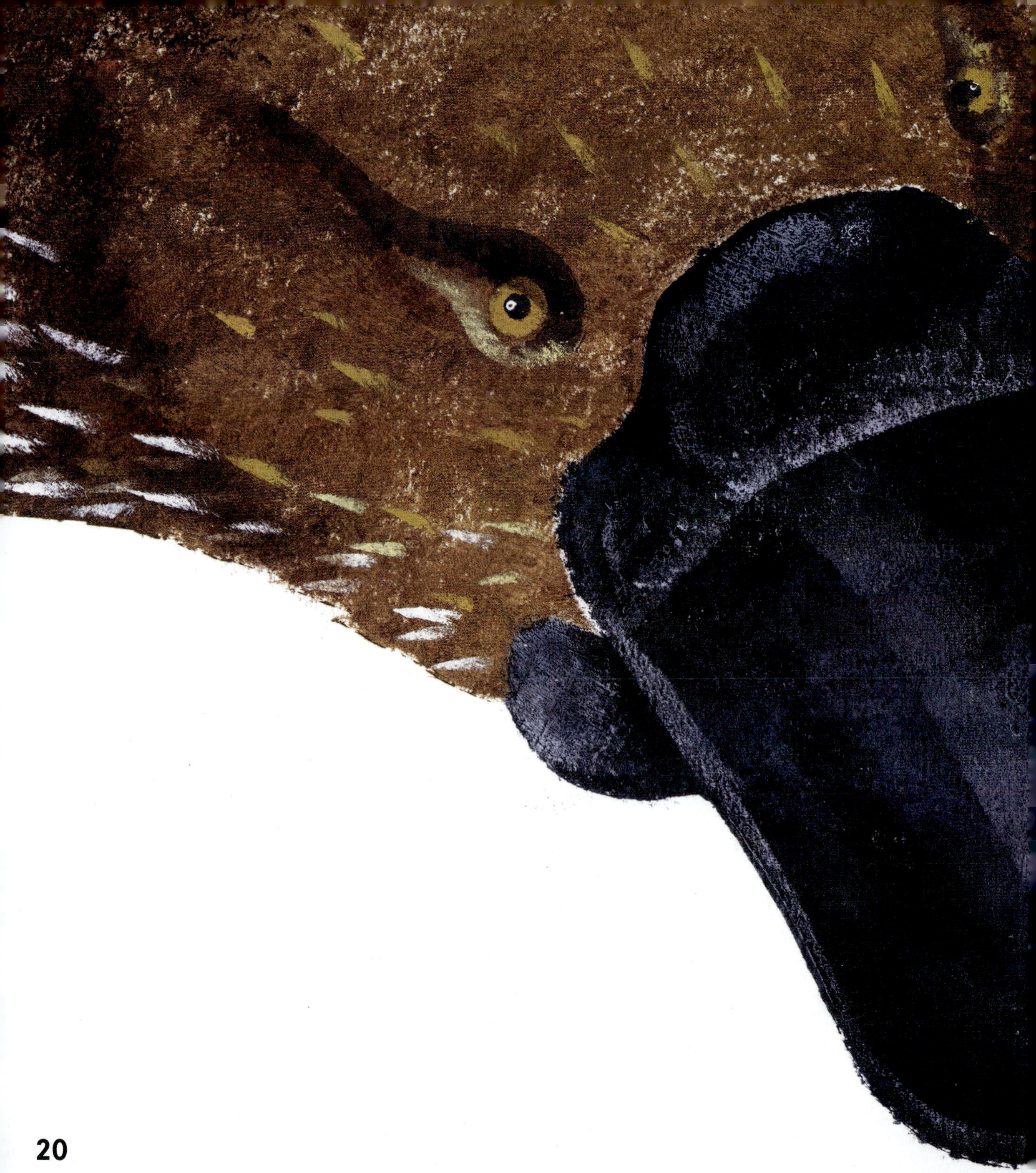

Whose Beak Is This?

Is it a duck?
Is it a goose?

This is not a bird's beak. It belongs to a **platypus!**

A platypus is a very unusual **mammal**. It has fur and it feeds its babies on milk like other mammals. But it also has a beak and lays eggs!

Platypuses use their beaks to find food in the water. They like to eat insects, tadpoles, shrimps and crayfish. They dive and swim underwater using their webbed feet.

These amazing animals live in Australia.

They look very cute and cuddly – but watch out! The male has **spurs** on his back legs that give a very painful sting.

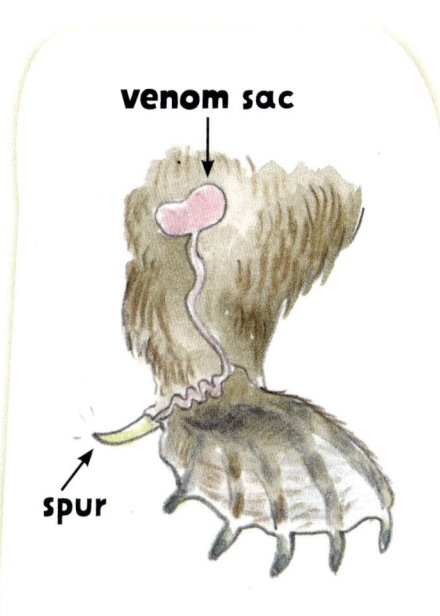

OUCH!

venom sac

spur

The male's spur is **venomous**.

23

Glossary

birds of prey: birds such as hawks or eagles that catch and eat other animals

breed: to have babies

breeding season: the time when an animal has its babies, often in the spring

burrows: tunnels or holes dug by animals to live in

colonies: groups of animals living together

mammal: an animal that usually gives birth to live babies and feeds them on milk

migration: when animals travel to different places for different seasons

predators: animals that hunt and eat other animals

prey: animals that are hunted and eaten by other animals

sap: a sticky liquid found in trees and plants

spurs: sharp spikes on a foot or leg

venom: a poison produced by an animal

venomous: able to inject venom by a bite or a sting

webbed feet: feet with toes that are joined together with pieces of skin

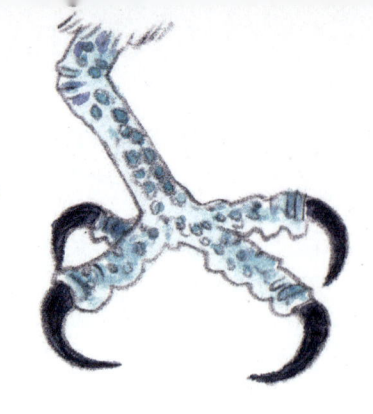

Index

breeding	6	platypus	22–23
mammal	22	predators	15
migration	11	puffin	6–7
osprey	10–11	venom	23
pelican	14–15	webbed feet	7, 15, 22
		woodpecker	18–19